I am Confucius

adapted by Gabriella DeGennaro

PENGUIN YOUNG READERS LICENSES
An Imprint of Penguin Random House LLC, New York

Published in 2021 by Penguin Young Readers Licenses, an imprint of Penguin Random House LLC, New York. Manufactured in China.

Visit us online at www.penguinrandomhouse.com.

ISBN 9780593224373   10 9 8 7 6 5 4 3 2

It was a quiet afternoon. Yadina sat cuddled up on the couch reading a book and eating some cheese and crackers.

Just as she was getting to a good part, Xavier marched into the room playing his recorder . . . *very* loudly.

"Can you *please* play somewhere else?" Yadina asked.

"The acoustics in here can't be beat," Xavier said, blowing a loud, funky tune.

Yadina frowned and popped one of the crackers into her mouth.

"Ooh! Can I have one?" Xavier asked.

Yadina pretended not to hear him, and with a loud *crunch*, gobbled up the last cracker.

Angrily, Xavier took a deep breath and blew his recorder into a microphone, sending his music blasting at full volume.

Just then, Brad walked in. "What is happening?" he asked.

Xavier and Yadina started shouting, blaming each other at the same time.

Brad could barely understand what was going on. He didn't want to say it, but he knew what he had to do.

"TO THE SECRET MUSEUM!" he yelled.

Xavier and Yadina froze in surprise.

"If the Secret Museum can get you to stop fighting, let's go," Brad said, as they raced off together.

They found a basket waiting for them on the podium.

"Look!" Brad said. "Confucius. That's who we're going to meet."

"In China in 543 BCE," Yadina said.

Brad's eyes widened in shock. "That means we're going back in time by . . . over two thousand years." He was dizzy just thinking about it.

Yadina wondered how Confucius was going to help. "Can he make *someone* play his recorder more quietly?" she asked.

"Or make *someone* better at sharing her snacks?" Xavier asked.

"Only one way to find out," Brad said. "Ready for adventure?"

"Hey, that's my line!" Xavier said.

Everyone placed their hands on Berby, and in a flash of light, they found themselves standing in a very wet and muddy rice field in China.

Brad felt dizzy from traveling so far back in time. Just as he was about to fall, someone swooped in to catch him.

"It's Confucius," Yadina whispered to her friends.
"Are you okay?" Confucius asked Brad.
"Oh! Yes, thanks," said Brad, grateful for his rescue.

Confucius gave a bow. "Happy to have helped," he said. "It's the rule I live by every day: Treat others how you would like to be treated. If I was about to fall in a wet rice field, I sure hope someone would catch me."

Next to Confucius was a heavy basket filled with games and snacks. He picked it up, ready to continue his walk. "It was nice meeting you," he said.

Brad noticed the basket matched the artifact from the Secret Museum. "Who's all that stuff for?" he asked, catching up to Confucius.

"My friend Mai. She's not feeling well," he explained.

"Did she ask for all this?" Xavier wondered.

"No, but like I said, treat others how you would like to be treated," Confucius said. "What if *you* were sick in bed? How would you like to be treated?"

When Brad was sick, he liked when his mom read to him. Yadina liked when Dr. Zoom was there to give her extra cuddles.

"I like it when my dad makes me chicken soup!" shared Xavier.

"So, you'd all like it if someone helped you," Confucius said.

"Me too! That's what I'm doing for my friend Mai."

Suddenly, Brad's stomach growled. The idea of warm chicken soup had made him hungry. Xavier and Yadina looked down at their rumbling tummies, too. This reminded them of the cheese and crackers, and soon they were fighting again.

"I'm happy to share my snack," Confucius said. "If I was hungry, and someone else had food, I sure hope they'd share it."

Yadina thought about how she had acted when her brother wanted her to share the crackers. *Treat others how you would like to be treated,* she thought to herself.

After they finished their snack, Confucius lifted the heavy basket and continued to lead the way to his friend's house.

Xavier spotted beautiful bells hanging from a wooden structure. "Check it out!" he called, running over to get a closer look.

Xavier picked up the mallet and hit the bells with all his might, and a very loud *DING* filled the air.

Confucius promised Xavier that they could go back and play the bells, but only after they dropped off the basket at Mai's.

The friends watched as Confucius, once again, lifted his heavy basket.

"Maybe we should help him," Brad said.

Yadina agreed, and the two of them rushed to catch up with him and lend a helping hand.

Xavier watched them go, staying behind.

He wanted to help, but he also wanted to stay and play the bells. Then he remembered: *Treat others how you would like to be treated.*

He imagined himself carrying something heavy, and how it would feel if no one helped him. Xavier knew just what to do.

He raced to catch up to his friends and helped carry the basket. Soon, they arrived at Mai's house.

"I'll be right back," Confucius said as he ran to meet his friend.

Xavier, Brad, and Yadina watched as she lit up with joy when Confucius shared the goodies in the basket.

Then Xavier spotted a new set of bells just waiting to be played. He reached for the mallet but paused just before playing, thinking of Mai, sick and trying to rest. "If I were trying to rest, I wouldn't like someone playing loud music," he said.

This made him think of Yadina trying to read.

"Yadina," he said, "I shouldn't have played so loudly when you were trying to read. I'm sorry."

"And I'm sorry, too," Yadina said. "I should have shared my snack."

The two of them hugged while Brad smiled wide. He knew it was time to go home.

Back in the living room, Yadina and Brad started reading her book. Xavier picked up his recorder from the coffee table. "I think I'll play this in another room," he said. "Quietly."

"That's very kind, Xavier." Yadina smiled. "Oh! But before you go . . ." She offered him a plate with cheese and crackers, happy to share her snack.